SUPER
SANDCASTLE
Super Simple Cooking

Super Simple
Snacks

Easy No-Bake Recipes for Kids

Nancy Tuminelly

Consulting Editor, Diane Craig, M.A./Reading Specialist

ABDO
Publishing Company

Published by ABDO Publishing Company, 8000 West 78th Street, Edina, Minnesota 55439. Copyright © 2011 by Abdo Consulting Group, Inc. International copyrights reserved in all countries. No part of this book may be reproduced in any form without written permission from the publisher. Super SandCastle™ is a trademark and logo of ABDO Publishing Company.

Printed in the United States of America, North Mankato, Minnesota
052010
092010

 PRINTED ON RECYCLED PAPER

Editor: Katherine Hengel
Content Developer: Nancy Tuminelly
Cover and Interior Design and Production: Colleen Dolphin, Mighty Media
Photo Credits: Colleen Dolphin, iStockphoto (Tammy Bryngelson, Dawna Stafford), Shutterstock
Food Production: Colleen Dolphin, Kelly Dolphin

The following manufacturers/names appearing in this book are trademarks:
Target® Plastic Wrap, Pyrex® Measuring Cup, Reynolds® Cut-Rite® Wax Paper,

Library of Congress Cataloging-in-Publication Data

Tuminelly, Nancy, 1952-
   Super simple snacks : easy no-bake recipes for kids / Nancy Tuminelly.
      p. cm. -- (Super simple cooking)
   ISBN 978-1-61613-388-7
   1. Snack foods--Juvenile literature. 2. Quick and easy cookery--Juvenile literature. I. Title.
   TX740.T85 2011
   641.5'39--dc22
                                    2009053190

Super SandCastle™ books are created by a team of professional educators, reading specialists, and content developers around five essential components—phonemic awareness, phonics, vocabulary, text comprehension, and fluency—to assist young readers as they develop reading skills and strategies and increase their general knowledge. All books are written, reviewed, and leveled for guided reading, early reading intervention, and Accelerated Reader® programs for use in shared, guided, and independent reading and writing activities to support a balanced approach to literacy instruction.

Note to Adult Helpers

Helping kids learn how to cook is fun! It is a great way for them to practice math and science. Cooking teaches kids about responsibility and boosts their confidence. Plus, they learn how to help out in the kitchen! The recipes in this book require very little adult assistance. But make sure there is always an adult around when kids are in the kitchen. Expect kids to make a mess, but also expect them to clean up after themselves. Most importantly, make the experience pleasurable by sharing and enjoying the food kids make.

Symbols

 knife
Always ask an adult to help you cut with knives.

keep it cold!
If you take this dish to go, use a cooler to keep it cold.

 nuts
Some people can get very sick if they eat nuts.

Contents

Let's Cook!

The recipes in this book are simple! You don't even need an oven or stove! Cooking teaches you about food, measuring, and following directions. It's fun to make good food! Enjoy your tasty creations with family and friends!

Bon appétit!

Cooking Basics

Before You Start...

- Get permission from an adult.
- Wash your hands.
- Read the recipe at least once.
- Set out all the ingredients, tools, and equipment you will need.
- Keep a towel close by for cleaning up spills.

When You're Done...

- Cover food with plastic wrap or **aluminum** foil. Use containers with tops when you can.
- Put all the ingredients and tools back where you found them.
- Wash all the dishes and **utensils**.
- Clean up your work space.

THINK SAFETY!

- Ask an adult to help you cut things. Use a cutting board.
- Clean up spills to prevent accidents.
- Keep tools and **utensils** away from the edge of the table or countertop.
- Use a **sturdy** stool if you cannot reach something.

Snack Attack!

Snacks are great! It's fun to take a break and have a special treat. But snacks can't take the place of real meals.

Be careful not to eat too many snacks during the day. You could spoil your dinner!

Reduce, Reuse, Recycle!

When it comes to helping the earth, little things add up! Here are some ways to go green in the kitchen!

• Reuse plastic bags. If they aren't too dirty, you can use them again!

• Take a lunchbox. Then you won't use a paper bag.

• Store food in reusable containers instead of using plastic bags.

• Carry a reusable water bottle. Then you won't buy drinks all the time!

Measuring Tips

Wet Ingredients
Set a measuring cup on the countertop. Add the liquid until it reaches the amount you need. Check the measurement from eye level.

Dry Ingredients
Dip the measuring cup or spoon into the dry ingredient. Scoop out a little more than you need. Use the back of a dinner knife to scrape off the **excess**.

Moist Ingredients
Ingredients like brown sugar and dried fruit are a little different. They need to be packed down into the measuring cup. Keep packing until the ingredient reaches your measurement line.

Do You Know This = That?

There are different ways to measure the same amount.

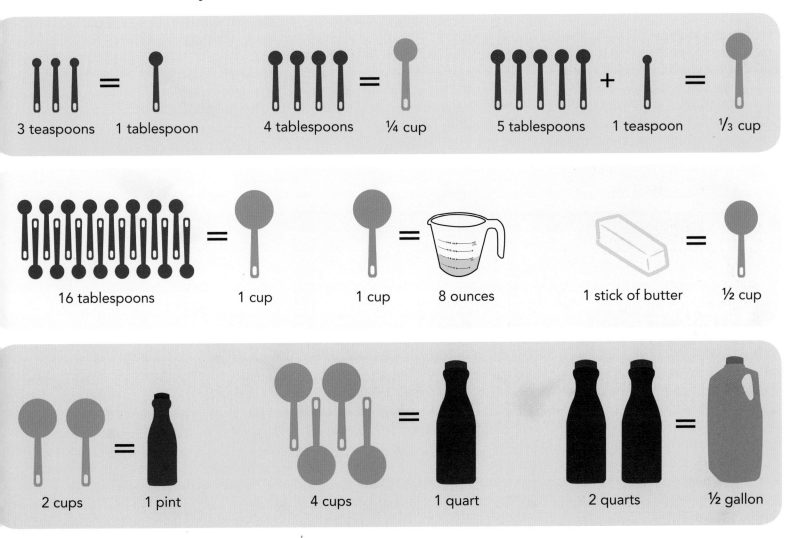

3 teaspoons = 1 tablespoon

4 tablespoons = ¼ cup

5 tablespoons + 1 teaspoon = ⅓ cup

16 tablespoons = 1 cup

1 cup = 8 ounces

1 stick of butter = ½ cup

2 cups = 1 pint

4 cups = 1 quart

2 quarts = ½ gallon

Cooking Terms

Arrange
Place food in a certain order or pattern.

Coat
Turn food gently to cover it with another ingredient.

Chop
Cut into very small pieces with a knife.

Dice
Cut into small cubes with a knife.

Drain
Remove liquid using a strainer or colander.

Grate
Shred food into small pieces with a grater.

Mash

Crush food until soft with fork or masher.

Mix

Combine ingredients with a mixing spoon.

Peel

Remove fruit or vegetable skin. Use peeler if needed.

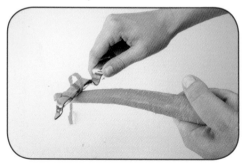

Pinch

Amount of an ingredient that can be held in fingers.

Keeping Food Fresh

Storing Food

Use **airtight** containers. They have tight lids to keep air out. Plastic zip top bags are good airtight containers too.

Covering Food

Use plastic wrap to cover food going in the refrigerator or on the countertop. Be careful not to put the plastic wrap on too tight. It can stick to your topping!

Tools

 Here are some of the tools that you'll need to get started.

can opener

vegetable peeler

plate

serving bowl

mixing bowls

cutting board

measuring cups
(dry ingredients)

measuring cup
(wet ingredients)

measuring spoons

grater

mixing spoon

plastic wrap

wax paper

spoon

fork

dessert cups

craft sticks

sharp knife

zip top sandwich bags

whisk

ice cream scoop

strainer

11

Ingredients

Fresh Produce

- ☐ lemons
- ☐ oranges
- ☐ bananas
- ☐ celery stalks
- ☐ carrots
- ☐ green peppers
- ☐ sweet onions
- ☐ cilantro
- ☐ parsley sprigs

Frozen

- ☐ frozen vanilla yogurt

Canned Goods

- ☐ tomatoes and chilies
- ☐ black-eyed peas
- ☐ chickpeas
- ☐ crushed pineapple

Meat

- ☐ sliced ham

Dairy

- ☐ sour cream
- ☐ cream cheese
- ☐ vanilla yogurt

Baking Aisle

- [ ] sugar
- [ ] granola
- [ ] dried basil
- [ ] nonfat dry milk powder
- [ ] raisins
- [ ] shredded coconut

Other

- [ ] banana chips
- [ ] peanuts
- [ ] dried cranberries
- [ ] sunflower seeds
- [ ] taco seasoning
- [ ] peanut butter
- [ ] honey
- [ ] guacamole
- [ ] Italian dressing

- [ ] tortilla chips
- [ ] lemon juice
- [ ] olive oil
- [ ] graham cracker crumbs
- [ ] craft sticks
- [ ] salt and pepper

Fruit Slurp Slushy

A refreshing drink you can eat!

Makes 4 servings

Ingredients

2 lemons

2 oranges

2 bananas, peeled

2 cups water

¾ cups sugar

Tools

- sharp knife
- cutting board
- mixing bowls
- fork
- mixing spoon
- measuring cups
- whisk
- plastic wrap
- dessert cups
- spoons

1 Roll lemons and oranges between your hand and countertop. Cut them in half and remove seeds. Squeeze juice from oranges and lemons into medium bowl.

 2 Mash bananas in small bowl with fork. Stir bananas and juices in large bowl with mixing spoon.

 3 Add water and sugar. Stir well with whisk until sugar is dissolved.

 4 Cover bowl with plastic wrap and put in freezer. Stir well every 20 minutes with whisk and return bowl to freezer. Do this for 1 hour.

 5 Serve when icy but not frozen solid. Pour into dessert cups and add spoons.

A juicer makes squeezing juice quick and easy! It's less messy too.

15

Cranberry Nut Crunch

Salty and sweet in one delicious mix!

Makes 6 servings

Ingredients

1 cup dried banana chips

2 cups peanuts

1 cup dried cranberries

1½ cups sunflower seeds

Tools

- measuring cups
- large mixing bowl
- mixing spoon
- ziptop bags or airtight containers

 1. Put all ingredients in large mixing bowl.

2. Mix well with mixing spoon.

3. Store leftovers in zip top bags or **airtight** containers. See page 9.

 Try adding 6 cups of popcorn to this snack mix!

1

2

3

17

Gorgeous Guacamole

This takes guacamole to the next level!

Makes 2 cups

Ingredients

8 ounces sour cream

8 ounces guacamole

2 tablespoons taco seasoning

tortilla chips

Tools

• measuring cups

• measuring spoons

• medium bowl

• mixing spoon

• plastic wrap

1. Put sour cream and guacamole in medium bowl. Stir well.

2. Add taco seasoning. Stir well.

3. Cover with plastic wrap. **Chill** for 1 hour. Serve with tortilla chips!

Peanut Butter Sticks

A healthy, sweet anytime treat!

Makes 4 servings

Ingredients

¼ cup peanut butter

½ cup honey

¼ cup granola

6 celery stalks, ends removed

Tools

- measuring cups
- mixing spoon
- small bowl
- spoon
- sharp knife
- cutting board

Mix peanut butter and honey together in small bowl.

 Use small spoon to fill center of celery stalks with peanut butter mixture.

 Sprinkle granola over peanut butter mixture.

 Cut stalks into smaller pieces and serve!

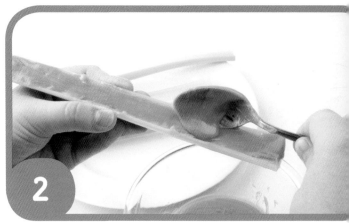

21

Tex-Mex Salsa

A super snack with a sassy kick!

Makes 4 servings

Ingredients

10-ounce can tomatoes and chilies

16-ounce can black-eyed peas, drained and rinsed

2 large green peppers, diced

1 cup sweet onion, diced

½ bunch cilantro, chopped

½ cup Italian dressing

tortilla chips

Tools

- can opener
- strainer
- mixing bowls
- sharp knife
- cutting board
- measuring cups
- mixing spoon
- plastic wrap
- serving bowls

Use strainer and large bowl to drain canned tomatoes and chilies. Discard juice.

 Mix all ingredients except tortilla chips in medium bowl. Cover with plastic wrap and **chill** for at least 2 hours.

 Place salsa in serving bowl. Serve with tortilla chips.

Carrot Top Canapés

A fun-to-make nutritious snack!

Makes 5 servings

Ingredients

14-ounce can chickpeas, drained

1 teaspoon lemon juice

1 tablespoon olive oil

¼ teaspoon dried basil

salt and pepper

2 tablespoons cream cheese

2 slices ham, chopped

2 cups carrots, peeled and grated

parsley sprigs

Tools

• can opener

• strainer

• fork

• large bowl

• measuring spoons

• mixing spoon

• sharp knife and cutting board

• vegetable peeler

• measuring cups

• grater

Mash chickpeas well in large bowl with fork.

 Stir in lemon juice, oil, basil, and a little salt and pepper.

 Mash cream cheese into mixture with fork.

 Add ham and 1 tablespoon carrots. Mix well with spoon. **Chill** 10 to 15 minutes.

 Form mixture into little carrot shapes. Coat each shape with grated carrots.

 Garnish with parsley **sprigs**.

Peanutty Power Balls

A power-packed, scrumptious snack!

Makes 8 servings

Ingredients

1 cup peanut butter

½ cup nonfat dry milk powder

½ cup raisins

¼ cup honey

1 cup graham cracker crumbs

Tools

- measuring cups
- medium bowl
- mixing spoon
- wax paper
- plate
- plastic wrap

1 Mix all ingredients except graham cracker crumbs in medium bowl.

2 Shape mixture into eight 1-inch balls and place on wax paper.

3 Coat balls with graham cracker crumbs. Place on clean plate. Cover in plastic wrap and **chill** for 1 hour before serving.

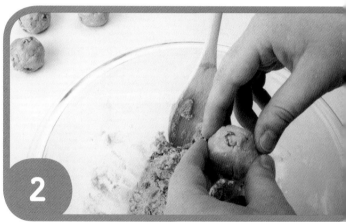

Coconut Delight

A sweet and crunchy snack!

Makes 6 servings

Ingredients

1 cup carrots, peeled and grated

1 cup crushed pineapple, drained

½ cup shredded coconut

½ cup raisins

3 cups of frozen vanilla yogurt

Tools

• vegetable peeler

• grater

• can opener

• strainer

• measuring cups

• medium mixing bowl

• mixing spoon

• ice cream scoop

• dessert cups

• plastic wrap

Mix all ingredients except yogurt in medium bowl.

 Cover with plastic wrap and **chill** for 30 minutes.

 Use ice cream scoop to place ½ cup frozen yogurt in six dessert cups. Top each one with ½ cup of chilled mixture.

 Try using your favorite yogurt flavor. You could even use cottage cheese instead!

Grahamy-Bananny Popsicles

A frozen treat that's great to eat!

Makes 2 servings

Ingredients

1 banana, peeled

2 craft sticks

6 ounces vanilla yogurt

½ cup graham cracker crumbs

Tools

• 2 craft sticks
• sharp knife
• cutting board
• two small bowls
• spoon
• wax paper
• plastic wrap

1 Cut banana in half **crosswise**. Push stick into flat end of each half.

 2 Put yogurt in small bowl. Coat banana with yogurt using a spoon.

3 Put graham crumbs in another bowl. Sprinkle graham crumbs onto banana until completely coated. Set on wax paper.

4 Cover with plastic wrap and freeze for at least 1 hour before serving.

Try honey or maple syrup instead of yogurt. Use coconuts, peanuts, granola, sesame seeds, or crushed chocolate wafer cookies instead of graham cracker crumbs.

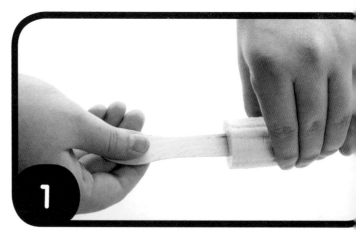

Glossary

airtight – so well sealed that no air can get in or out.

aluminum – a light metal.

chill – to put something in the refrigerator to make it cold or firm.

crosswise – in the direction of the shortest side.

excess – more than the amount wanted or needed.

garnish – to decorate with small amounts of food.

sprig – a small bit of grass or herbs, usually used as a garnish.

sturdy – strong and well built.

utensil – a tool used to prepare or eat food.